The Kingman Comprehension Series

Intermediate Level 6

Dr. Alice Kingman

PARTRIDGE

ISBN: Softcover   978-1-5437-7407-8
             eBook   978-1-5437-7408-5

Print information available on the last page.

To order additional copies of this book, contact
Toll Free +65 3165 7531 (Singapore)
Toll Free +60 3 3099 4412 (Malaysia)
orders.singapore@partridgepublishing.com

www.partridgepublishing.com/singapore

Contents

Acknowledgements

First, I would like to thank Jazzy, the illustrator of the Kingman Comprehension Series, for her beautiful artistic drawings which bring every story she has worked on to life.

My great appreciation is also to be extended to my two daughters, Stephanie and Audrey, who helped me from the very beginning in the typing and formatting of questions for every reading passage.

A big thank you to my beloved husband, Matt, for his continuous support, encouragement, and professional assistance in the computerised structuring of the book.

I am also grateful to all my students for their contributions to this project, working on different passages, testing out questions, and providing invaluable feedback.

With no reservation, my heartfelt gratitude goes to my beloved late father, Joseph, who spared no effort in teaching me English since I was seven years old.

Thank you to all other members of my family who spurred me on to take this big step in realising my dreams of becoming an English-language author. I thank them for their love and patience throughout the whole process. Thank you to my wonderful church family as well for their uplifting prayers and support.

Last but not least, I thank God, my Heavenly Father, every day for His unfailing presence and spiritual guidance, without which this project would not have happened.

To Teacher and Parent

In my lifelong career as an English-language teacher, I have often been disappointed and discouraged to find questions set for comprehension passages stressing speedy location of answers or meticulous reproduction of the text. The formulated questions seldom encourage students to read between the lines or genuinely understand the writer's choice of diction and intention of writing. In other words, students are often deprived of opportunities to think out of the box and explore implied meanings and examine the purpose of sentence structure.

Hence, it has always been my ambition to produce a comprehension series that can sharpen students' skills in analytical discernment. The Kingman Comprehension Series comprises high-interest selections of different literary genres, from classics to renowned children's literature, including fables, folk and fairy tales, poems, legends, myths, as well as modern realistic fictions. It is my hope that students will find the works of the outstanding authors in the books not only enjoyable to work on but also interesting enough to spark further independent reading amongst themselves.

Adventures of Huckleberry Finn

Mark Twain

"And besides, if you will I'll show you my sore toe."

Jim was only human--this attraction was too much for him. He put down his pail, took the white alley, and bent over the toe with absorbing interest while the bandage was being unwound. In another moment he was flying down the street with his pail and a tingling rear, Tom was whitewashing with vigor, and Aunt Polly was retiring from the field with a slipper in her hand and triumph in her eye.

But Tom's energy did not last. He began to think of the fun he had planned for this day, and his sorrows multiplied. Soon the free boys would come tripping along on all sorts of delicious expeditions, and they would make a world of fun of him for having to work--the very thought of it burnt him like fire. He got out his worldly wealth and examined it--bits of toys, marbles, and trash; enough to buy an exchange of WORK, maybe, but not half enough to buy so much as half an hour of pure freedom. So he returned his straitened means to his pocket, and gave up the idea of trying to buy the boys. At this dark and hopeless moment an inspiration burst upon him! Nothing less than a great, magnificent inspiration.

He took up his brush and went tranquilly to work. Ben Rogers hove in sight presently--the very boy, of all boys, whose ridicule he had been dreading. Ben's gait was the hop-skip-and-jump--proof enough that his heart was light and his anticipations high. He was eating an apple, and giving a long, melodious whoop, at intervals, followed by a deep-toned ding-dong-dong, ding-dong-dong, for he was personating a steamboat. As he drew near, he slackened speed, took the middle of the street, leaned far over to starboard and rounded to ponderously and with laborious pomp and circumstance--for he was personating the Big Missouri, and considered himself to be drawing nine feet of water. He was boat and captain and engine-bells combined, so he had to imagine himself standing on his own hurricane-deck giving the orders and executing them:

"Stop her, sir! Ting-a-ling-ling!" The headway ran almost out, and he drew up slowly toward the sidewalk.

"Ship up to back! Ting-a-ling-ling!" His arms straightened and stiffened down his sides.

"Set her back on the stabboard! Ting-a-ling-ling! Chow! ch-chow-wow! Chow!" His right hand, mean-time, describing stately circles--for it was representing a forty-foot wheel.

"Let her go back on the labboard! Ting-a-ling-ling! Chow-ch-chow-chow!" The left hand began to describe circles.

Answer the following questions.

1. Jim was attracted to see the other boy's _____ _____.

2. Which idiom (four words in the second paragraph) tells us that Jim was moving fast?

3. What caused Jim's sorrow to be multiplied?

4. "The very thought of it burnt him like fire" is an example of
   a. a rhyme   b. a simile   c. a metaphor   d. personification

5. What were the "straitened means" in the third paragraph referring to?

6. Which line tells us that Tom's idea was an amazing one?

7. Tom started to execute his plan by taking up his brush and going tranquilly to work. What do you think Tom's intention for doing that was?

8. If there was one boy Tom dreaded the most, it was _____ _____ who was at that moment pretending to be a _____ called the _____ _____.

9. What did Ben's animated gait and sounds prove?

10. What was Ben Rogers not pretending to be?
    a. the boat   b. the water   c. the captain   d. the engine bells

11. Arrange the following sentences in the correct sequence:
    _____ Aunt Polly succeeded in making Tom work.
    _____ Jim watched the unwinding of the bandage round the toe.
    _____ Ben directed the boat back.
    _____ Tom started running out of steam.

12. Would you enjoy spending a day with Jim, Tom and Ben? Explain.

Read on:

Adventures of Huckleberry Finn, a novel by American author Mark Twain, was first published in December 1884. Known for its colourful descriptions of people and places, the story is told from the point of view of Huck Finn, who runs away from an abusive, drunken father and later encounters a runaway slave called Jim, and Tom Sawyer, the nephew of the Phelps family.
With themes of racism, freedom, civilization and prejudice being examined, the book ultimately proves significant as a novel that explores the moral world of its time and the modern day.

A Princess of Mars

Edgar Rice Burroughs

I am a very old man; how old I do not know. Possibly I am a hundred, possibly more; but I cannot tell because I have never aged as other men, nor do I remember any childhood. So far as I can recollect I have always been a man, a man of about thirty. I appear today as I did forty years and more ago, and yet I feel that I cannot go on living forever; that some day I shall die the real death from which there is no resurrection. I do not know why I should fear death, I who have died twice and am still alive; but yet I have the same horror of it as you who have never died, and it is because of this terror of death, I believe, that I am so convinced of my mortality. And because of this conviction I have determined to write down the story of the interesting periods of my life and of my death. I cannot explain the phenomena; I can only set down here in the words of an ordinary soldier of fortune a chronicle of the strange events that befell me during the ten years that my dead body lay undiscovered in an Arizona cave.

I have never told this story, nor shall mortal man see this manuscript until after I have passed over for eternity. I know that the average human mind will not believe what it cannot grasp, and so I do not purpose being pilloried by the public, the pulpit, and the press, and held up as a colossal liar when I am but telling the simple truths which some day science will substantiate. Possibly the suggestions which I gained upon Mars, and the knowledge which I can set down in this chronicle, will aid in an earlier understanding of the mysteries of our sister planet; mysteries to you, but no longer mysteries to me.

My name is John Carter; I am better known as Captain Jack Carter of Virginia. At the close of the Civil War I found myself possessed of several hundred thousand dollars (Confederate) and a captain's commission in the cavalry arm of an army which no longer existed; the servant of a state which had vanished with the hopes of the South. Masterless, penniless, and with my only means of livelihood, fighting, gone, I determined to work my way to the southwest and attempt to retrieve my fallen fortunes in a search for gold.

Answer the following questions.

1. The writer of this story believes he is over _____ _____ years old.

2. Why can't the writer tell exactly how old he is?

3. True or False:
   a. The writer has died before and is still alive. _____
   b. The writer is not afraid of death. _____

4. The expression "this conviction" in the first paragraph refers to
   a. the writer's belief that he will truly die one day
   b. the writer's determination to write down what has happened

5. Where has the dead body of the writer been laid in the previous ten years?

6. When does the writer want people to know about what has happened to him?

7. Match the following words with the correct definitions:

   resurrection   a formal document to vest someone with authority
   mortality   a written record of historical events
   phenomenon   the state of being subject to death
   chronicle   a remarkable happening
   commission   the rising of the dead

8. In the part of the sentence "and so I do not purpose being pilloried by the public, the pulpit, and the press...", the literary device employed is
   a. personification   b. alliteration   c. repetition

9. The writer is waiting for _____ to prove what has happened to him is real.

10. What is the sister planet in the second paragraph referring to?

11. The writer resorts to search for gold because
    a. he has very little money left
    b. he loves gold
    c. he likes the southwestern part of the United States

12. This kind of writing is in the realm of
    a. fiction   b. non-fiction   c. history

Read on:

Written by Edgar Rice Burroughs, *A Princess of Mars* follows the exciting saga of John Carter, a Virginian Civil War veteran who finds himself in the midst of some rival tribes on the red planet, Mars. When his captors take the lovely princess of the city of Helium as prisoner, John summons up all his strength and courage to rescue her.

The Wind

Robert Louis Stevenson

I saw you toss the kites on high

And blow the birds about the sky;

And all around I heard you pass,

Like ladies' skirts across the grass--

O wind, a-blowing all day long,

O wind, that sings so loud a song!

I saw the different things you did,

But always you yourself you hid.

I felt you push, I heard you call,

I could not see yourself at all--

O wind, a-blowing all day long,

O wind, that sings so loud a song!

O you that are so strong and cold,

O blower, are you young or old?

Are you a beast of field and tree,

Or just a stronger child than me?

O wind, a-blowing all day long,

O wind, that sings so loud a song!

Answer the following questions.

1. In the first verse "I saw you toss the kites on high", the pronoun "you" is referring to _____ _____.

2. What is the passing of the wind compared to?

3. Quote the verses to show that the poet could not see where the wind was.

4. The wind is described to be able to "push" and "call." These are examples of
   a. a simile
   b. alliteration
   c. personification

5. True or False:
   a. The poet is asking if the wind was strong and cold. _____
   b. The poet is asking if the wind was young or old. _____

6. When the wind is strong and roaring loud, it is compared to a _____.

7. What is not an example that shows the poet is conscious of the presence of the wind?
   a. The wind tosses a kite high.
   b. The wind helps the birds fly in the sky.
   c. The wind moves across the lake.

8. Is the narrator of this poem a child or an adult? Give evidence.

9. Which two verses are repeated throughout the poem?

10. What is the rhyme scheme of this poem?

11. Do you like this poem? Why or why not?

12. Name another famous poem written by Robert Louis Stevenson.

Read on:

In the poem 'The Wind', Robert Louis Stevenson is eager to express his curiosity towards the wind from the point of view of a child.

'The Wind' is a three-stanza poem divided into sets of six lines known as sestets, following a rhyme scheme of closed couplets. Poetic techniques like enjambment, caesura, personification and alliteration are employed to convey the nature of this common element called the wind.

The Secret Garden

Francis Hodgson Burnett

Mary went back to her room not feeling at all as she had felt when she had come in from the garden. She was cross and disappointed but not at all sorry for Colin. She had looked forward to telling him a great many things and she had meant to try to make up her mind whether it would be safe to trust him with the great secret. She had been beginning to think it would be, but now she had changed her mind entirely. She would never tell him and he could stay in his room and never get any fresh air and die if he liked! It would serve him right! She felt so sour and unrelenting that for a few minutes she almost forgot about Dickon and the green veil creeping over the world and the soft wind blowing down from the moor.

Martha was waiting for her and the trouble in her face had been temporarily replaced by interest and curiosity. There was a wooden box on the table and its cover had been removed and revealed that it was full of neat packages.

"Mr. Craven sent it to you," said Martha. "It looks as if it had picture-books in it."

Mary remembered what he had asked her the day she had gone to his room. "Do you want anything—dolls—toys—books?" She opened the package wondering if he had sent a doll, and also wondering what she should do with <u>it</u> if he had. But he had not sent one. There were several beautiful books such as Colin had, and two of them were about gardens and were full of pictures. There were two or three games and there was a beautiful little writing-case with a gold monogram on it and a gold pen and inkstand.

Everything was so nice that her pleasure began to crowd her anger out of her mind. She had not expected him to remember her at all and her hard little heart grew quite warm.

"I can write better than I can print," she said, "and the first thing I shall write with that pen will be a letter to tell him I am much obliged."

Answer the following questions.

1. Mary had been _____ _____ _____ seeing Colin but was now _____ and _____ with him.

2. How do we know that Mary was very upset with Colin? Circle the correct statements.
   a. She would never tell him the news.
   b. She would not allow Colin to stay in his room.
   c. She wouldn't mind if Colin died.

3. Which sentence tells us that Mary felt Colin deserved to suffer for disappointing her?

4. The phrase "the green veil creeping over the world" is an example of
   a. alliteration   b. a simile   c. hyperbole

5. On seeing Mary, Martha became _____ and _____ temporarily.

6. What did Mary first see on opening the wooden box? Why was she able to see them?

7. Change the following sentence to indirect speech. "Mr. Craven sent it to you," said Martha. "It looks as if it had picture-books in it."
   Martha said that _____
   _____.

8. What is "it" underlined in the fourth paragraph referring to?

9. Name any four items that were found in the wooden box.

10. What were the two reasons why Mary brightened up on opening the box?

11. The expression "I am much obliged" in the last paragraph suggests that Mary was
    a. grateful   b. troubled   c. unappreciative

12. Arrange the following sentences in the correct sequence:
    _____ Mary felt touched by the presents she received.
    _____ Mary felt upset with Colin.
    _____ Mary met up with Martha.
    _____ Mary visited Mr. Craven in his room.

Read on:
In the novel *The Secret Garden* by Francis Hodgson Burnett, Mary Lennox is a lonely, unloved child born into luxury.
On finding a locked secret garden in her new home in Yorkshire Moors, Mary starts interacting with nature, navigates through life with friends and being transformed to a much happier, kinder and better person.

The Little Prince

Antoine de Saint-Exupéry

Once when I was six years old I saw a magnificent picture in a book, called *True Stories from Nature*, about the primeval forest. It was a picture of a boa constrictor in the act of swallowing an animal. Here is a copy of the drawing.

In the book it said: "Boa constrictors swallow their prey whole, without chewing it. After that they are not able to move, and they sleep through the six months that they need for digestion."

I pondered deeply, then, over the adventures of the jungle. And after some work with a coloured pencil I succeeded in making my first drawing. My Drawing Number One. It looked something like this:

I showed my masterpiece to the grown-ups, and asked them whether the drawing frightened them.

But they answered: "Frighten?" Why should any one be frightened by a hat?"

My drawing was not a picture of a hat. It was a picture of a boa constrictor digesting an elephant. But since the grown-ups were not able to understand it, I made another drawing: I drew the inside of a boa constrictor, so that the grown-ups could see it clearly. They always need to have things explained. My Drawing Number Two looked like this:

The grown-ups response, this time, was to advise me to lay aside my drawings of boa constrictors, whether from the inside or the outside, and devote myself instead to geography, history, arithmetic and grammar. That is why, at the age of six, I gave up what might have been a magnificent career as a painter. I had been disheartened by the failure of my Drawing Number One and my Drawing Number Two. Grown-ups never understand anything by themselves, and it is tiresome for children to be always and forever explaining things to them.

So then I chose another profession, and learned to pilot airplanes. I have flown a little over all parts of the world; and it is true that geography has been very useful to me. At a glance I can distinguish China from Arizona. If one gets lost in the night, such knowledge is valuable.

In the course of this life I had had a great many encounters with a great many people who have been concerned with matters of consequence. I have lived a great deal among grown-ups. I have seen them intimately, close at hand. And that hasn't much improved my opinion of them.

Answer the following questions.

1. When the writer was _____ years old, he saw a _____ picture about the _____ forest.

2. A synonym for "primeval" in the first paragraph is
   a. prehistoric
   b. valuable
   c. modern

3. Why would a boa constrictor need to sleep through six months after swallowing a prey?

4. Underline the two words in the third paragraph which mean "thought for a long time".

5. The word _____ suggests that the writer was very proud of his drawing.

6. Were the grown-ups frightened by Drawing Number One? Why or why not?

7. What did the grown-ups advise the writer to study? How are these subjects different from drawing?

8. Which was not a criticism of the grown-ups by the writer?
   a. Grown-ups always need to have things explained to them.
   b. Children find grown-ups difficult to love.
   c. Grown-ups never understand anything by themselves.

9. Did the writer take the advice of the grown-ups? How do you know?

10. Which subject did the writer take that proved to be most useful to him as he grew up? Explain.

11. From the final paragraph, we learn that the writer's opinion of grown-ups hadn't improved much. What was that opinion?

12. The story *The Little Prince* was translated from French to English. What clue suggests it was first written in French?

Read on:

The Little Prince, authored by French writer Antoine de Saint-Exupéry and published in 1943, follows the trips made by a young prince who visits various unique planets, including our planet, Earth. The story is recalled by the pilot-navigator in memory of his special new-found friend. Translated into over 250 languages, *The Little Prince* remains one of the most read books in schools as a teaching tool for learning other languages.

Five Children and It

Edith Nesbit

It was at the gravel-pits. Father had to go away suddenly on business, and Mother had gone away to stay with Granny, who was not very well. They both went in a great hurry, and when they were gone the house seemed dreadfully quiet and empty, and the children wandered from one room to another and looked at the bits of paper and string on the floors left over from the packing, and not yet cleared up, and wished they had something to do. It was Cyril who said—

"I say, let's take our spades and dig in the gravel-pits. We can pretend it's seaside."

"Father says it was once," Anthea said; "he says there are shells there thousands of years old."

So they went. Of course they had been to the edge of the gravel-pit and looked over, but they had not gone down into it for fear Father should say they mustn't play there, and it was the same with the chalk-quarry. The gravel-pit is not really dangerous if you don't try to climb down the edges, but go the slow safe way round by the road, as if you were a cart.

Each of the children carried its own spade, and took it in turns to carry the Lamb. He was the baby, and they called him that because "Baa" was the first thing he ever said. They called Anthea "Panther," which seems silly when you read it, but when you say it, it sounds a little like her name.

The gravel-pit is very large and wide, with grass growing round the edges at the top, and dry stringy wildflowers, purple and yellow. It is like a giant's washbowl. And there are mounds of gravel, and holes in the sides of the bowl where gravel has been taken out, and high up in the steep sides there are the little holes that are the little front doors of the little bank-martins' little houses.

The children built a castle, of course, but castle-building is rather poor fun when you have no hope of the swishing tide ever coming in to fill up the moat and wash away the drawbridge, and, at the happy last, to wet everybody up to the waist at least.

Cyril wanted to dig out a cave to play smugglers in, but the others thought it might bury them alive, so it ended in all spades going to work to dig a hole through the castle to Australia. These children, you see, believed that the world was round, and that on the other side the little Australian boys and girls were really walking wrong way up, like flies on the ceiling, with their heads hanging down into the air.

Answer the following questions.

1. The children were left alone at home because Father had to leave all of a sudden to do _____ and Mother had to visit _____ who was _____.

2. Was the house clean and tidy? Explain.

3. Give two reasons why Cyril suggested they should go and dig in the gravel-pits.

4. What were the two places Father would not like the children to play in?

5. The phrase "as if you were a cart" is an example of
   a. a simile
   b. a metaphor
   c. personification

6. What was the baby called? Why?

7. Was "Panther" an appropriate name for Anthea? Explain.

8. Match the gravel-pit with the correct descriptions:

   a. was large and wide.
   b. had only grass growing around it.
   The gravel-pit
   c. had piles of gravel in the sides of the basin.
   d. was always filled with water.
   e. was the home of a giant.

9. What two conditions, according to the writer, would make building a castle fun?

10. What was Cyril's suggestion? Was it well supported by the others? Why or why not?

11. In what way would, according to the children, the Australian boys and girls be like flies on the ceiling?

12. Another suitable title for this story would be
    a. Irresponsible Parents
    b. Mischievous Children
    c. A Dreary Day
    d. Children at Play

Read on:

In the children's novel *Five Children and It* written by English writer Edith Nesbit, four children and their baby brother are playing in a gravel pit when they discover an ugly, grumpy sand-fairy with the ability to grant wishes. Every day, each child is granted a wish that lasts until sunset, but often with disastrous consequences.

Bambi's Children

Felix Salten

"It's Faline, the roe-deer! Faline and her children!"

Crows came flapping from their nests.

"Faline!" they echoed disapprovingly. "She spoils her children. They have their own way in everything. Disgraceful!"

Faline turned her quiet brown eyes upward to the treetops.

"You see, Geno," she said, "what <u>they</u> think of me? Now, be a good boy and stop whining."

"But I'm tired. I want to lie down," Geno complained.

"He's not a bit tired!" His sister, Gurri, trotted close to her mother's red-brown flanks. "It's just because I ran faster than he did when I played his stupid old game. He's an old sorehead!"

"I'm not a sorehead, and you can't run as fast as I can! You're just a girl, that's all you are … !"

"I'd like to know what that's got to do with it!" Gurri tossed her head and a shower of dewdrops fell gleaming from a low-hanging bush.

"Children!" Faline remonstrated soothingly.

"Well, Mother, if he wasn't such a spoilsport! Boso and Lana wanted to go in playing, but he," she mimicked him disparagingly, "he was so tired!"

Angrily Geno drummed his small hoofs on the winding path.

"You'll see! I won't show you any more games!"

"All right, I'll make up my own!"

"You will!"

"All right, Boso will! He's cleverer than you are and he's nice!"

The crows flew away with great flapping of black wings.

"You see? What did we tell you!" they croaked scornfully. "Just listen to those children!"

"Nasty black things!" Geno scoffed. "If my father, Bambi, were here, he'd show you!"

"Ho, ho, ho!" chortled the crows. "Teach him manners, Faline!"

A woodpecker paused in his drumming at an old oak tree.

"That's it, Faline," he cried shrilly; "otherwise he'll have no friends when he needs them."

"The woodpecker's giving good advice," Faline told her son, but Geno interrupted her. He leaped away from the path-side, jostling his sister.

Answer the following questions.

1. What kind of animal is Faline?

2. Why didn't the crows like Faline?

3. In the question "You see, Geno," she said, "what they think of me?", whom is "they" referring to?

4. What do you think is the relationship between Faline and Geno?

5. Gurri thought Geno was not really tired when Geno said he was. What did Gurri think the real reason was?

6. Geno's "an old sorehead" means Geno is
    a. a hurtful person
    b. a bad-tempered person
    c. a stubborn person

7. When Geno said, "You're just a girl, that is all you are ......!", he is being a bit biased against the _____ gender.

8. What fell from a low-hanging bush when Gurri tossed her head?

9. Was the path that Geno drummed his hoofs on a straight path? Explain.

10. Who is the speaker of the line "All right, I'll make up my own!"
    It means he/she will make up his/her own _____.

11. Match the following adverbs to the correct meanings:
    a. disapprovingly   i. disrespectfully
    b. soothingly   ii. gently
    c. scornfully   iii. critically

12. Words like "drummed" his small hoofs and "croaked" scornfully are examples of
    a. a rhyme
    b. onomatopoeia
    c. a simile

Read on:

Bambi's Children, the Story of a Forest Family, was written by Austrian author Felix Salten as a sequel to his earlier work *Bambi, a Life in the Woods*.

In the story, Geno and Gurri, the twin fawns of Faline and Bambi, explore the world of the wood where they grow up to be adult deer, learning along the way the pleasures and drawbacks of their forest home with the help and guidance of their mother.

Rebecca of Sunnybrook Farm

Kate Douglas Wiggin

"Stop, uncle Jerry! Don't turn in at the side; hand me my satchel, please; drop me in the road and let me run up the path by myself. Then drive away quickly."

All the noise and rumble of the approaching stage the house door opened from within, just as Rebecca closed the gate behind her. Aunt Jane came down the stone steps, a changed woman, frail and broken and white. Rebecca held out her arms and the old aunt crept into <u>them</u> feebly, as she did on that day when she opened the grave of her buried love and showed the dead face, just for an instant, to a child. Warmth and strength and life flowed into the <u>aged frame</u> from the young one.

"Rebecca," she said, raising her head, "before you go in to look at her, do you feel any bitterness over anything she ever said to you?"

Rebecca's eyes blazed reproach, almost anger, as she said chokingly: "Oh, Aunt Jane! Could you believe it of me? I am going in with a heart brimful of gratitude!"

"She was a good woman, Rebecca; she had a quick temper and a sharp tongue, but she wanted to do right, and she did it as near as she could. She never said so, but I'm sure she was sorry for every hard word she spoke to you; she didn't take 'em back in life, but she acted so 't you'd know her feeling when she was gone."

"I told her before I left that she'd been the making of me, just as Mother says," sobbed Rebecca.

"She wasn't that," said Jane. "God made you in the first place, and you've done considerable yourself to help Him along; but she gave you the <u>wherewithal</u> to work with, and that ain't to be despised; specially when anybody gives up her own luxuries and pleasures to do it. Now let me tell you something, Rebecca. Your Aunt Miranda's willed all this to you – the brick house and buildings and furniture, and that land all round the house, as far 's you can see."

Rebecca threw off her hat and put her hand to her heart, as she always did in moments of intense excitement. After a moment's silence she said: "Let me go in alone; I want to talk to her; I want to thank her; I feel as if I could make her hear and feel and understand!"

Answer the following questions.

1. In what ways was Jane a "changed" woman?

2. What is the pronoun "them" underlined in the second paragraph referring to?

3. The "aged frame" in the second paragraph is referring to Aunt Jane. This literary technique is called:
   a. a simile   b. alliteration   c. metonymy

4. What did Aunt Jane worry about before letting Rebecca enter the house to see her (Aunt Miranda) - the "good" woman?

5. Which word between the third and fifth paragraphs tells us that Rebecca almost cried?

6. What were the shortcomings of Aunt Miranda according to Aunt Jane?

7. True or False:
   It was believed that Aunt Miranda
   a. wanted to do right _____
   b. was ready to apologize _____
   c. wanted Rebecca to understand her feelings one day _____

8. The word "wherewithal" in the seventh paragraph means
   a. money and means
   b. time and attention
   c. knowledge and wisdom

9. Why shouldn't Rebecca despise what Aunt Miranda had given her?

10. When would Rebecca get the brick house, building, furniture and the land round the house? Which word tells you that?

11. Two of the themes of this passage are
    a. gratitude
    b. repentance
    c. generosity

12. Give another title to this part of the story.

Read on:

Eleven-year old Rebecca Randall, an impulsive and carefree child, is leaving her beloved Sunnybrook Farm to live with her two stern but well-to-do aunts and get an education. The story follows the girl's growth and maturing into a young lady who charms everyone she comes across. More than a hundred years after its first publication, *Rebecca of Sunnybrook Farm* remains a firm favourite with children and adults all around the world.

Donal That Was Rich and Jack That Was Poor

Seamas MacManus

At length Donal began to suspect that Jack was taking his bullocks, but he didn't know how he would find out for sure. Donal's old mother-in-law proposed a plan by which she could catch Jack. She made Donal put her into a big chest that had little spy-holes in it, and put in with her beef and brandy enough to last her nine days. Then Donal was to take the chest to Jack's, and have it left there on some excuse.

Donal went to Jack, and said he had a big chest of things that was in his way, and asked Jack if he would be so good as to allow him to leave it in his kitchen for a week or so. Jack said he was very welcome to put in ten chests if he liked. So Donal had the chest with the mother-in-law and her provisions in it, carried to Jack's, and planted in a good place in the kitchen.

On the very first night that the chest and the mother-in-law were at Jack's, he stole and killed and brought in another bullock, and the old woman was watching it all through the spy-holes of the chest. And after Jack and his wife and children had eaten a hearty supper off the bullock, he and his wife began talking over one thing and another, and he said: "I'd like to know what Donal has in that chest."

So off he went to a locksmith, and he got the loan of a whole bundle of keys, and he came and tried them all in the chest till he got one that opened it.

When Jack found what was in the chest, he lost little time taking away the beef and brandy, and he put in their place empty bottles and clean-picked bones, and locked the old woman up with these again.

At the end of nine days, Donal came for the chest. He thanked Jack for giving him house room for it for so long, and said he had now room for it himself and so he had come to take it home. And behold you, when Donal and his wife opened the chest at home, there was the old woman dead of starvation, and a lot of bones and empty bottles in the chest.

Says Donal: "She got greedy, and ate and drank the whole of the provisions the first day, and this is her deserving."

Well, Donal and the wife waked and buried her, with a purse of money, under her head to pay her way in the next world, as they used to do in those days.

Jack, of course, he went to the wake and to the funeral, and sympathized sore with Donal and Donal's wife both.

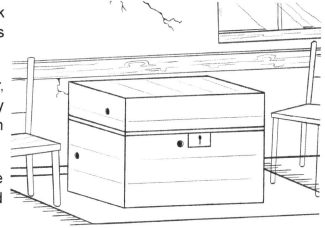

Answer the following questions.

1. _____ _____ proposed a plan to catch Jack.

2. How could the old woman see Jack hiding in the chest?

3. Write the plural forms of these words:
   a. mother-in-law   _____
   b. beef   _____
   c. excuse   _____
   d. spy-hole   _____

4. Underline the sentence that shows us Jack did not mind keeping the chest.

5. Did Jack want to find out what was in the chest immediately after his family had eaten supper? Explain.

6. A hearty supper means
   a. a full supper   b. a warm supper   c. a modest supper

7. Change the following sentence to indirect speech. "I'd like to know what Donal has in that chest," said Jack.
   Jack said _____.

8. Could Jack open the chest in one try? Explain

9. Underline the expression (three words between the fourth and sixth paragraphs) which means "wasted no time".

10. What were in the chest when Jack unlocked it?

11. Write the nouns of the following words:
    a. suspect _____
    b. provide _____
    c. starve _____
    d. deserve _____

12. What was the purse of money for?

Read on:

From the Seamus MacManis book *Donegal Fairy Tales*, 'Donal That Was Rich and Jack That Was Poor' is a story of two brother's mischievous maneuvering over their differences in wealth. Suspicious of Jack's taking the bullocks from Donal's herd, Donal's old mother-in-law proposes a plan by which she could catch Jack red-handed. However, Jack continues to outwit his brother until the latter makes Jack's family a very happy and wealthy one.

Around the World in Eighty Days

Jules Verne

But Mr. Fogg, far from being discouraged, was continuing his search, resolved not to stop if he had to resort to stop if he had to resort Macao, when he was <u>accosted</u> by a sailor on one of the wharves.

"Is your honour looking for a boat?"

"Have you a boat ready to sail?"

"Yes, your honour; a pilot-boat – No. 43 – the best in the harbour."

"Does <u>she</u> go fast?"

"Between eight and nine knots the hour. Will you look at her?"

"Yes."

"Your honour will be satisfied with her. Is it for a sea excursion?"

"No, for a voyage."

"A voyage?"

"Yes, will you agree to take me to Yokohama?"

The sailor leaned on the railing, opened his eyes wide, and said, "Is your honour joking?"

"No. I have missed the *Carnatic*, and I must get to Yokohama by the 14th at the latest, to take the boat for San Francisco."

"I am sorry," said the sailor, "but it is impossible."

"I offer you a hundred pounds per day, and an additional reward of two hundred pounds if I reach Yokohama in time."

"Are you earnest?"

"Very much so."

The pilot walked away a little distance, gazed out to sea, evidently struggling between the anxiety to gain a large sum and the fear of venturing so far. Fix was in mortal suspense.

Mr. Fogg turned to Aouda and asked her, "You would not be afraid, would you, madam?"

"Not with you, Mr. Fogg," was her answer.

The pilot now returned, shuffling his hat in his hands.

"Well, pilot?" said Mr. Fogg.

"Well, your honour," replied he, "I could not risk myself, my men, or my little boat of scarcely twenty tons on so long a voyage at this time of year. Besides, we could not reach Yokohama in time, for it is sixteen hundred and sixty miles from Hong Kong."

"Only sixteen hundred," said Mr. Fogg.

"It's the same thing."

Answer the following questions.

1. Was Mr. Fogg losing hope in looking for a vessel? Underline the phrase (four words in the first ten lines) that supports your answer.

2. Was Macao a place Mr. Fogg wanted to visit initially? Explain.

3. An antonym for the verb "accosted" is
   a. ignored   b. confronted   c. attacked

4. Change to indirect speech. The sailor asked, "Is your honour looking for a boat?"
   The sailor asked _____.

5. Mr. Fogg asked the sailor, "Does <u>she</u> go fast?"
   The pronoun "<u>she</u>" is referring to the _____.

6. Use the two words "excursion" and "voyage" in the correct context.
   a. The _____ across the Pacific Ocean could be rough at times.
   b. Our science teacher is taking us on a/an _____ up the mountain.

7. Why did the sailor open his eyes wide?

8. True or False:
   a. Mr. Fogg missed the *Carnatic* and ended up in Yokohama. _____
   b. Mr. Fogg wanted to go to San Francisco via Yokohama. _____
   c. Mr. Fogg decided to stay where he was. _____

9. What did Mr. Fogg offer the sailor for the arrangement?

10. What was the sailor's dilemma?

11. What reasons did the sailor give for not taking up the offer?
    a. He did not want to risk his own life.
    b. He did not want to risk the lives of his men.
    c. He did not want to lose his little boat.
    d. They could not reach Yokohama in time.

12. Mr. Fogg corrected the sailor, saying that Yokohama is only sixteen hundred miles, and not sixteen hundred and sixty miles, from Hong Kong. Why did he do that?

Read on:
One of Jules Vernes' most acclaimed works, *Around the World in Eighty Days* is an adventure novel that follows the dramatic attempt of Phileas Fogg of London and his newly hired French emotional valet, Passpartout, to travel around the world in 80 days on a placed bet of £20,000. The places visited were mostly British colonies: Egypt, Yemen, India, Singapore, Hong Kong and Ireland, reflecting the vastness of the British Empire at that time (1872) in history.

Chatterer the Red Squirrel Runs for his Life

Thornton W. Burgess

<u>Chatterer the Red Squirrel</u> had been scolding because there was no excitement. He had even tried to make some excitement by waking <u>Bobby Coon</u> and making him so angry that Bobby had threatened to eat him alive. It had been great fun to dance around and call Bobby names and make fun of him. Oh, yes, it had been great fun. You see, he knew all the time that Bobby couldn't catch him if he should try. But now things were different. Chatterer had all the excitement that he wanted. Indeed, he had more than he wanted. The truth is, Chatterer was running for his life, and he knew it.

It is a terrible thing, a very terrible thing to have to run for one's life. <u>Peter Rabbit</u> knows all about it. He has run for his life often. Sometimes it has been <u>Reddy Fox</u> behind him, sometimes <u>Bowser the Hound</u>, and once or twice <u>Old Man Coyote</u>. Peter has known that on his long legs his life has depended, and more than once a terrible fear has filled his heart. But Peter has also known that if he could reach the old stone wall or the dear <u>Old Briar</u>-patch first, he would be safe, and he always has reached it. So when he has been running with that terrible fear in his heart, there has always been hope there, too.

But Chatterer the Red Squirrel was running without hope. Yes, Sir, there was nothing but fear, terrible fear, in his heart, for he knew not where to go. The hollow tree or the holes in the old stone wall where he would be safe from any one else, even Farmer Brown's boy, offered him no safety now, for the one who was following him with hunger in his anger-red eyes could go anywhere that he could go--could go into any hoe big enough for him to squeeze into. You see, it was <u>Shadow the Weasel</u> from whom Chatterer was running, and Shadow is so slim that he can slip in and out of places that even Chatterer cannot get through.

Chatterer knew all this, and so, because it was of no use to run to his usual safe hiding places, he ran in just the other direction. He didn't know where he was going. He had just one thought: to run and run as long as he could and then, well, he would try to fight, though he knew it would be of no use.

"Oh, dear! Oh, dear!" he sobbed, as he ran out on the branch of a tree and leaped across to the next tree. "I wish I had minded my own business! I wish I had kept my tongue still. Shadow the Weasel wouldn't have known where I was if he hadn't heard my voice. Oh, dear! oh, dear me! What can I do? What can I do?"

Now in his great fright Chatterer had run and jumped so hard that he was beginning to grow very tired. Presently he found that he must make a very long jump to reach the next tree. He had often made as long a jump as this and thought nothing of it, but now he was so tired that the distance looked twice as great as it really was. He didn't dare stop to run down the tree and scamper across. So he took a long breath, ran swiftly along the branch, and leaped.

Answer the following questions.

1. Chatterer was complaining because there had been _____ _____.

2. How did Chatterer usually annoy Bobby Coon?

3. Why was Chatterer not afraid of Coon's taking revenge?

4. Underline the expression (four words in the first paragraph) which means "running very fast."

5. Has Peter Rabbit run for his life before? Give evidence.

6. The characters Chatterer was afraid of were
   a. Bowser the Hound
   b. Reddy Fox
   c. Bobby Coon
   d. Old Man Coyote

7. When Chatterer ran for his life, what was his heart usually filled with?.

8. In the current situation, Chatterer's heart was only filled with _____ because
   _____.

9. Why could Shadow the Weasel skip in and out of holes easily?

10. Tick the two correct answers.
    "Oh, dear! Oh, dear!" is an example of
    a. repetition
    b. interjection
    c. conjunction

11. Which word tells us Chatterer was so scared that he was in tears?

12. What regrets did Chatterer have? Does it have anything to do with his name?

Read on:
In this story, you will find Chatterer the Squirrel getting in trouble again and is forced to leave his old home in search of a new one.
Chatterer's curiosity and carelessness causes him to stumble into a place very different from what he originally expects to find. The personalities, behaviour and mischievousness of the different species of animals are delightfully described by author Thornton W. Burgess (1874-1965).

The Phoenix and the Carpet

Edith Nesbit

"I don't know any sweet-smelling wood, except cedar," said Robert; "but I've got some ends of cedar-wood lead pencil."

So they burned the ends of lead pencil. And still nothing happened.

"Let's burn some of the eucalyptus oil we have for our colds," said Anthea.

And they did. It certainly smelt very strong. And they burned lumps of camphor out of the big chest. It was very bright, and made a horrid black smoke, which looked very magical. But still nothing happened. Then they got some clean tea-cloths from the dresser drawer in the kitchen, and waved them over the magic chalk-tracings, and sang 'The Hymn of the Moravian Nuns at Bethlehem', which was very impressive. And still nothing happened. So they waved more and more wildly, and Robert's tea-cloth caught the golden egg and whisked it off the mantelpiece, and it fell into the fender and rolled under the grate.

"Oh, crikey!" said more than one voice.

And every one instantly fell down flat on its front to look under the grate, and there lay the egg, glowing in a nest of hot ashes.

"It's not smashed, anyhow," said Robert, and he put his hand under the grate and picked up the egg. But the egg was much hotter than any one would have believed it could possibly get in such a short time, and Robert had to drop it with a cry of "Bother!" It fell on the top bar of the grate, and bounced right into the glowing red-hot heart of the fire.

"The tongs!" cried Anthea. But, alas, no one could remember where they were. Every one had forgotten that the tongs had last been used to fish up the doll's teapot from the bottom of the water-butt, where the Lamb had dropped it. So the nursery tongs were resting between the water-butt and the dustbin, and cook refused to lend the kitchen ones.

"Never mind," said Robert, "we'll get it out with the poker and the shovel."

"Oh, stop," cried Anthea. "Look at it! Look! Look! Look! I do believe something *is* going to happen!"

For the egg was now red-hot, and inside it something was moving. Next moment there was a soft cracking sound; the egg burst in two, and out of it came a flame-coloured bird. It rested a moment among the flames, and as it rested there the four children could see it growing bigger and bigger under their eyes.

Every mouth was a-gape, every eye a-goggle.

The bird rose in its nest of fire, stretched its wings, and flew out into the room. It flew round and round, and round again, and where it passed the air was warm. Then it perched on the fender. The children looked at each other. Then Cyril put out a hand towards the bird. It put its head on one side and looked up at him, as you may have seen a parrot do when it is just going to speak, so that the children were hardly astonished at all when it said, "Be careful; I am not nearly cool yet."

Answer the following questions.

1. The children burned ends of _____ lead pencils, _____
   _____ and lumps of _____ but nothing happened.

2. What is the pronoun "them" underlined in the fourth paragraph referring to?

3. Find a word which means "frantically" in the fourth paragraph.

4. What happened when the children waved the tea-cloths more and more excitedly?

5. "Oh, crikey!" is an adjective/adverb/interjection which is an Australian expression of disbelief/
   sadness/sympathy.

6. What did the children see when they looked under the grate?

7. True or False:
   a. Robert dropped the egg and smashed it. _____
   b. Robert dropped the egg because it was too hot. _____

8. Where were the nursery tongs that the children wanted to fetch?

9. Underline the part of the sentence in the eighth paragraph that infers the cook was not
   cooperative.

10. How many times did Anthea say "Look"? Why?

11. Underline the sentence in the last three paragraphs that tells us that all the children were
    shocked. What had they seen?

12. What part of this story can be true? What part of this story cannot be true?

Read on:

In the story *The Phoenix and the Carpet* by Edith Nesbit, five children are playing when they find
an egg lying in the new carpet their mother has just bought. The egg hatches into a talking phoenix
which explains the carpet is a magic one that will grant them three wishes a day.

The children's adventures are continued and concluded in the third book of the trilogy *The Story
of the Amulet* published in 1906.

The Old Wife and the Ghost

James Reeves

There was an old wife and she lived all alone
In a cottage not far from Hitchin;
And one bright night, by the full moon light,
Comes a ghost right into her kitchen.

About that kitchen neat and clean
The ghost goes pottering round.
But the poor old wife is deaf as a boot
And so hears never a sound.

The ghost blows up the kitchen fire,
As bold as can be;
He helps himself from the larder shelf,
But never a sound hears she.

He blows his hands to make them warm,
And whistle aloud "Whee-hee!"
But still as a sack the old soul lies
And never a sound hears she.
From corner to corner he runs about,
And into cupboards he peeps;
He rattles the door and bumps on the floor,
But still the old wife sleeps.

Jangle and bang go the pots and pans,
As he throws them all around;
And the plates and mugs and dishes and jugs,
He flings them all to the ground.

Madly the ghost tears up and down
And screams like a storm at sea;
And at last the old wife stirs in her bed-
And it's "Drat those mice", says she.

Then the first cock crows and morning shows
And the troublesome ghost's away.
But oh! What a pickle the poor wife sees
When she gets up next day.

'Them's tidy big mice', the old wife thinks
And off she goes to Hitchin,
And a tidy big cat she fetches back
To keep the mice from her kitchen.

Answer the following questions.

1. What kind of poem is this?
   a. a descriptive poem
   b. a narrative poem
   c. a haiku

2. Did the old wife live with her family? How do you know?

3. What lit up the town of Hitchin that particular night?

4. The verse "About that kitchen neat and clean" is an example of a poetic device called
   a. enjambment
   b. inversion
   c. personification

5. The poor old wife cannot hear because she is as _____ as a _____. This is an example of a poetic technique called a simile/metaphor.

6. Where is the food of the old wife stored?

7. Underline the verse which tells us that the old wife doesn't move at all.

8. An onomatopoeia is a word formed from a sound associated with what is named. Which of the following is not an example of this poetic device?
   a. rattles
   b. jangle
   c. bang
   d. pickle

9. Use an adjective to describe the ghost? Why does he behave like that?

10. When does the ghost leave? Why does he do that?

11. What does the old wife buy to solve the problem? Why does she do that?

12. The purpose of this poem is to
    a. entertain
    b. complain
    c. give advice

Read on:
A poem written by James Reeves, 'The Old Wife and the Ghost' tells the story of an old lady who lives alone in the house and a ghost tries to scare her by banging on doors and windows and throwing kitchen utensils on the floor. However the lady is deaf, and on getting up the next morning and seeing the mess made, she blames the mice for it and brings in a cat.

Marcus or, The Boy-Tamer The Troublesome Scholar

Walter Aimwell

THERE was one boy in the academy who still caused Marcus no little anxiety. His name was Harrison Clark, and he was about fourteen years old, and large for his age. This was his first term at the academy. He was from an adjoining town, and but little was known of him, except what he himself chose to divulge. The achievement of his short life upon which he seemed to pride himself most, was a fight he had with his former teacher, a month or two before this, in which, according to his representation, he came off victor; and he had been heard to threaten a similar infliction upon Marcus, should that personage attempt to chastise him. One or two of the elder pupils were anxious that the insolence of this pert young gentleman should be <u>checked</u> by a sound thrashing, and they even intimated to the teacher that aid would not be wanting, in case the boy should offer serious resistance. But Marcus thought there was a more excellent way to subdue him, and determined to try it, before resorting to harsh measures.

Marcus happened one day to fall in with a townsman of Harrison, from whom he gathered all the information he could in regard to the career and character of the boy. It appeared that he had been governed with severity, both at home and at school, so far as he had been governed at all. He had steadily grown worse, however, under this discipline, and his parents, finding they could do nothing with him, had sent him away to school, as the easiest way to rid themselves of a constant trouble. They were finally led to this course, by his altercation with his teacher. Several boys, it seemed, got into a wild frolic in the school-room, one day, before the opening of the session, in the course of which Harrison threw an inkstand at another lad, by which his face and clothes were stained, and the walls, floor, and seats soiled. The teacher, after investigating the matter, ordered Harrison to hold out his hand for punishment, which he refused to do, in an insolent manner. The teacher then attempted to seize his hand, but failing in this, he tripped the boy upon the floor, and a regular scuffle ensued. Another boy, still larger than Harrison, now rushed to the assistance of the latter, and before the disgraceful affray ended, they inflicted two or three serious blows upon the teacher, and then fled. They were both arrested for assault, and after a trial before a justice, were fined, Harrison ten dollars and the other boy five, besides the cost of the trial, which was divided between them. While it must be confessed that their punishment was just, I think few will deny that the teacher also was to be blamed for the part he acted in the affray.

Answer the following questions.

1. Harrison Clark brought Marcus
    a. much comfort
    b. much trouble
    c. much satisfaction

2. True or False:
    a. Harrison looked like he was sixteen or seventeen years old in size. _____
    b. Harrison was always ready to tell others about himself. _____

3. What do you think caused Harrison to be expelled from his former school?

4. Harrison threatened Marcus "with a similar infliction." That means Harrison threatened to
    _____ _____ Marcus.

5. The word "checked" underlined in the first paragraph means
    a. stopped
    b. guarded
    c. examined

6. We learn that Harrison sometimes acted like an animal because he needed to be _____.

7. From whom did Marcus learn about the career and character of Harrison?

8. The speculation that Harrison was "governed with severity" means his parents
    a. guided him along patiently
    b. treated him like a prince
    c. were very strict with him

9. What did Harrison's parents do when they knew they had failed to raise him properly?

10. What were the immediate consequences of Harrison's throwing an inkstand at another boy?

11. Who was injured most badly in the fight that involved a number of individuals?

12. True or False:
    Harrison and the other boys were fined fifteen dollars in total. _____
    Explain.

Read on:

The story, *Marcus or, the Boy-Tamer* written by Walter Aimwell, is written to portray some of the phases of juvenile character and to point out how their tendencies to future good and evil can be affected by incidents that occur at home and abroad, at school and in the open playground.

The Story of the Second Old Man, and the Two Black Dogs

(The Arabian Nights)

Great prince of the genii, you must know that we are three brothers—these two black dogs and myself. Our father died, leaving us each a thousand sequins. With this sum we all three took up the same profession, and became merchants. A short time after we had opened our shops, my eldest brother, one of these two dogs, resolved to travel in foreign countries for the sake of merchandise. With this intention he sold all he had and bought merchandise suitable to the voyages he was about to make. He set out, and was away a whole year. At the end of this time a beggar came to my shop. "Good-day," I said. "Good-day," he answered; "is it possible that you do not recognise me?" Then I looked at him closely and saw he was my brother. I made him come into my house, and asked him how he had fared in his enterprise.

"Do not question me," he replied, "see me, you see all I have. It would but renew my trouble to tell of all the misfortunes that have befallen me in a year, and have brought me to <u>this state</u>."

I shut up my shop, paid him every attention, taking him to the bath, giving him my most beautiful robes. I examined my accounts, and found that I had doubled my capital—that is, that I now possessed two thousand sequins. I gave my brother <u>half</u>, saying: "Now, brother, you can forget your losses." He accepted them with joy, and we lived together as we had before.

Some time afterwards my second brother wished also to sell his business and travel. My eldest brother and I did all we could to dissuade him, but it was of no use. He joined a caravan and set out. He came back at the end of a year in the same state as his elder brother. I took care of him, and as I had a thousand sequins to spare I gave them to him, and he re-opened his shop.

One day, my two brothers came to me to propose that we should make a journey and trade. At first I refused to go. "You travelled," I said, "and what did you gain?" But they came to me repeatedly, and after having held out for five years I at last gave way. But when they had made their preparation, and they began to buy merchandise we needed, they found they had spent every piece of the thousand sequins I had given them. I did not reproach them. I divided my six thousand sequins with them, giving a thousand to each and keeping one to myself, and the other three I buried in a corner of my house. We bought merchandise, loaded a vessel with it, and set forth with a favourable wind.

After two months' sailing we arrived at a seaport, where we disembarked and did a great trade.

Then we bought merchandise of the country, and were just going to sail once more, when I was stopped on the shore by a beautiful though poorly dressed woman. She came up to me, kissed my hand, and implored me to marry her, and take her on board. At first I refused, but she begged so hard and promised to be such a good wife to me, that at last I consented.

Answer the following questions.

1. Who were the three brothers as mentioned at the beginning of the story?

2. What did the eldest brother want to do?

3. Could the merchant recognize his eldest brother immediately? Explain.

4. "This state" in the second paragraph refers to the state of being _____ _____.

5. How much is "half" as mentioned in the third paragraph?

6. Which word in the fourth paragraph suggests that the merchant and his eldest brother tried to talk the second brother into not selling his business and travel? Were they successful?

7. How did the two elder brothers try to get the merchant to give in to their suggestion?

8. Two antonyms for the word "reproach" are
   a. praise
   b. scold
   c. lecture harshly
   d. compliment

9. Where did the merchant bury the remaining three thousand sequins?

10. The repetition of the letter "f" used in "and set forth with a favourable wind" is an example of
    a. repetition
    b. alliteration
    c. contradiction

11. Could the three brothers sell their merchandise well at the seaport? Explain.

12. One would probably not like to have two brothers like the ones the merchant has. Explain.

Read on:

'The Story of the Second Old Man, and the Two Black Dogs', the third story found in *One Thousand and One Nights*, describes three brothers who have received a large inheritance from their father. The second old man, the generous one, becomes a hardworking shop owner but his two other brothers, on the other hand, squander all their money and convince their honest brother to go on a trading trip with them. Jealous of their brother's success, they even plot to kill both the brother and his wife in the sea for their wealth.

The Coming of Pollyanna

Eleanor H. Porter

In due time came the telegram, announcing that Pollyanna would arrive in Beldingsville the next day, the twenty-fifth of June, at four o'clock. Miss Polly read the telegram, frowned, then climbed the stairs to the attic room. She still frowned as she looked about her.

The room contained a small bed, neatly made, two straight-backed chairs, a washstand, a bureau – without any mirror – and a small table. There were no drapery curtains at the dormer windows, no pictures on the wall. All day the sun had been pouring down upon the roof, and the little room was like an oven for heat. As there were no screens, the windows had not been raised. A big fly was buzzing angrily at one of <u>them</u> now, up and down, trying to get out.

Miss Polly killed the fly, swept it through the window (raising the sash an inch for the purpose), straightened a chair, frowned again, and left the room.

"Nancy," she said a few minutes later, at the kitchen door, "I found a fly up-stairs in Miss Pollyanna's room. The window must have been raised at some time. I have ordered screens, but until they come I shall expect you to see that the windows remain closed. My niece will arrive tomorrow at four o'clock. I desire you to meet her at the station. Timothy will take the open buggy and drive you over. The telegram says 'light hair, red-checked gingham dress, and straw hat.' That is all I know, but I think it is sufficient for your purpose."

"Yes, ma'am; but – you – "

Miss Polly evidently read the pause aright, for she frowned and said crisply:

"No, I shall not go. It is not necessary that I should, I think. That is all." And she turned away – Miss Polly's arrangements for the comfort of her niece, Pollyanna, were complete.

In the kitchen, Nancy sent her flat iron with a vicious dig across the dish-towel as she was ironing.

"'Light hair, red-checked gingham dress, and straw hat' – all she knows, indeed! Well, I'd be ashamed ter own it up, that I would, I would – and her my onliest niece what was a-comin' from 'way across the continent!"

Promptly at twenty minutes to four the next afternoon Timothy and Nancy drove off in the open buggy to meet the expected guest. Timothy was Old Tom's son. It was sometimes said in the town that if Old Tom was Miss Polly's right-hand man, Timothy was her left.

Timothy was a good-natured youth, and a good-looking one, as well. Short as had been Nancy's stay at the house, the two were already good friends. Today, however, Nancy was too full of her mission to be her usual talkative self; and almost in silence she took the drive to the station and alighted to wait for the train.

Over and over in her mind she was saying it "light hair, red-checked dress, straw hat." Over and over again she was wondering just what sort of child this Pollyanna was, anyway.

Answer the following questions.

1. Miss Polly learned of Pollyanna's arrival by _____.

2. What was the date Miss Polly received the notice?

3. Was Pollyanna's room fully furnished? Explain.

4. Pollyanna's room, which was hot because of the sun, was compared to _____ _____.

5. What is "them" underlined in the second paragraph referring to?

6. True or False:
   a. Miss Polly let the fly out of the window. _____
   b. Miss Polly ordered Nancy to open the windows until the screens arrived. _____

7. Did Miss Polly know her niece well? Which two sentences support your answer?

8. How many times was the word "frowned" used in the passage?
   That implies Miss Polly was excited / anxious / guilty about Pollyanna's arrival.

9. Was Nancy frustrated by the instructions given by Miss Polly? Find evidence to support your answer.

10. How many nieces did Miss Polly have? How do you know?

11. Were Old Tom and Timothy, in the eyes of the town folk, great assistants to Miss Polly? Explain.

12. Does this story take place in old or modern days? Give evidence.

Read on:

Pollyanna, a best selling novel written by Eleanor H. Porter in 1913, follows the story of the young protagonist who comes to a town inhabited by bitter folks. She confronts its attitude with boldness and determination, refusing to be depressed but to remain positive and see the best of life—a frame of mind she has learned from her late father.
It is believed by many that Pollyanna has ascended her status as a fictional character to become a recognizable personality type that is characterized by irrepressible optimism and a tendency to find good in everything.

The Pied Piper of Hamelin

Robert Browning

The good citizens of Hamelin weren't too sure about that but they went home to their houses to see what would be done. But nothing was done. There was just as much rubbish in the street and just as many rats in the mills, the bakeries, the shops and the houses. In fact there were more rats. The rats kept growing and breeding and breeding and growing and eating and eating and eating.

They ate anything they could get their teeth on. Nothing or no one was safe from the rats.

The people were angry and marched to the Town Square and pounded on the big brass doors and to know exactly what the Lord Mayor was going to do. When no Lord Mayor appeared on the balcony. The people started to chant.

"No rats!" "No rats!" "No rats!"

Finally the Lord Mayor appeared on the balcony in his black robes and gold chains and announced somewhat nervously that he had a definite plan of action.

"Good citizens of Hamelin you will be pleased to know that I, the Lord Mayor, have given ordered that a large hole in the ground will be dug on the outskirts of Hamelin and into that hole will be swept all of the rubbish in the streets and all of the rats that can be found and killed. Soon Hamelin will be clean and clear of rats."

Soon the large hole in the ground was full of stinking rubbish and the bodies of dead rats and hurriedly covered over with dirt. But it was not enough there were too many rats in too many hiding places all over the town and too much food for them in the silos and bakeries and shops and houses and they grew and bred and bred and grew just as fast as before. And now with the rats came a plague of fleas. And with the fleas came a strange sickness. Some children and old people had already died. A plague was on Hamelin!

As you can imagine the people of Hamelin were even angrier. They marched once more to the town square. Each of them carried with them a dozen dead rats as proof of the failure of the Lord Mayors plan. They threw the rats in a pile in the middle of the square and from a pole they hung an effigy that looked remarkably like the Lord Mayor in his black robes and his gold chains. They started chanting-

"No Rats or no Mayor!" "No Rats or no Mayor!" "No Rats or no Mayor!"

When the Lord Mayor did come out on his balcony he was surrounded by his Councillors and he announced rather nervously that the council had, in view of the rather desperate situation, agreed to offer a magnificent reward of one thousand gold guilders to any person who could rid the town of the rats.

The very next day a stranger appeared in Hamelin. He was different to everyone else. His clothes were colourful and seemed to come from many different places. He wore a hat covered with feathers and shells and bones. From a long scarf hung a silver pipe.

Answer the following questions.

1. Underline the sentence in the first paragraph which suggests that all the citizens of Hamelin would be disappointed.

2. Tick the correct sentence:
   _____ There was more rubbish than there were rats.
   _____ There were more rats than there was rubbish.
   _____ The amount of rubbish and the number of rats were the same.

3. How do we know the rats ate anything they could find?

4. Which word (between the third and sixth paragraphs) tells us the Lord Mayor was not calm? _____

5. What was the solution the Lord Mayor first suggested to the citizens of Hamelin to get rid of the rats?

6. Which was not a reason why the rats could not be gotten rid of?
   a. There were too many hiding places.
   b. Too much food could be found.
   c. There was a plague.

7. Arrange the following sentences in the correct sequence:
   _____ Some children and old people died.
   _____ The rats brought about a plague of fleas.
   _____ A hole was dug for burying rubbish and dead rats.
   _____ The fleas brought about a strange sickness.

8. What shows that the people were really upset with the failure of the Lord Mayor?

9. Which was more serious a threat?
   a. "No rats!"   b. "No rats or no Mayor!"

10. How do we know the Lord Mayor was not alone when he appeared on the balcony the second time?

11. Was the sum promised to any person who could rid the town of rats a handsome amount? Which three words suggest that?

12. Which of the following items do you think will be crucial to the development of the story? Refer to the 'Read on' section.
    a. the hat   b. the scarf   c. the cart   d. the silver pipe

Read on: Dating back to the Middle Ages, *The Pied Piper of Hamelin*, is also known as *The Pied Piper* or *The Rat-Catcher of Hamelin*.
A piper, dressed in a multicoloured outfit, is hired to lure the thousands upon thousands of rats away with his magic pipe. When his service is not paid for, he retaliates by leading one hundred and thirty children of the town into a cave, after which they have not been seen again. The most popular version ends with a child who is lame and cannot follow the procession returning to inform the villagers what has happened.

Pride and Prejudice

Jane Austen

Chapter 15 - Elizabeth Receives a Letter

Elizabeth woke the next morning to the same thoughts. It was impossible to fix her mind on anything else, so she decided soon after breakfast to give herself air and exercise. She was going directly towards her favourite part of the park, when she remembered that Mr. Darcy sometimes came there, and she turned up the narrow road outside Rosings.

After a little time she caught sight of a gentleman within the dark. She had turned away, but when she heard a voice calling her, though it was Mr. Darcy's, she moved towards the gate. He, too, had reached it by this time. Holding out a letter, he said, with a look of proud calm, 'Will you do me the honour of reading this?' Then he turned and was soon out of sight.

Elizabeth opened the letter and saw two sheets, completely covered in handwriting. The letter had been written at Rosings, at eight o'clock in the morning, and read as follows:

Do not be troubled, madam, on receiving this letter. I write without any intention of upsetting you, or wounding my own self-respect, by mentioning unnecessarily what passed between us last night. But my character demands this to be written and read. You must, therefore, pardon the freedom with which I ask your attention. You will, I know, give it unwittingly, but I must request it as a matter of justice.

Last night, you charged me with two offences of a very different kind. The first was that I had separated Mr. Bingley from your sister, and the other that I had ruined the hopes of Mr. Wickham. I must now explain these matters.

I had not been in Hertfordshire for long before I saw that Bingley preferred your oldest sister to any other young woman there. I did not take this seriously, because I had often seen him in love before. But at the ball at Netherfield, while I had the honour of dancing with you, I first realized, through Sir William Lucas's accidental information, that Bingley's attentions to your sister had caused a general expectation that they would be married. From that moment I watched my friend carefully, and saw that his attraction to Miss Bennet was beyond what I had ever seen in him before. I also watched your sister. Her look and manner were open, cheerful and pleasing as well, but I saw no signs of strong feeling. If *you* have not been mistaken here, I must have been deceived. Your greater knowledge of your sister makes it probable that you were right.

Answer the following questions.

1. Elizabeth, on waking up, decided to go for a walk for some _____ and _____.

2. What made Elizabeth turn up the narrow road outside Rosings?

3. True or False:
   a. Elizabeth stopped on hearing Mr. Darcy's voice. _____
   b. Elizabeth and Mr. Darcy reached the gate at almost the same time. _____

4. Underline the phrase (six words in the second paragraph) which suggests that Mr. Darcy was not shy or flustered on seeing Elizabeth.

5. Match the following statements correctly with the characters:

	a. had the letter written in Rosings.
Elizabeth	b. was being handed a letter.
Mr. Darcy	c. read the letter as requested.
	d. wrote the letter at eight o'clock in the morning.

6. Was the letter short and sweet? Support your answer with two pieces of evidence.

7. What was probably the intention of the letter?
   a. to upset Elizabeth
   b. to wound the self respect of Darcy
   c. to explain what had transpired between Darcy and Elizabeth

8. Mr. Darcy demanded the letter to be written and read as he saw it as _____ _____ _____ _____.

9. What were the offences Mr. Darcy was charged with?

10. Why didn't Mr. Darcy initially take Mr. Bingley's affection for Miss Bennet seriously?

11. Why didn't Mr. Darcy take Miss Bennet's response to Mr. Bingley seriously?

12. What do you think Elizabeth would feel after reading the letter?
    a. less burdened by unclarified thoughts
    b. more sympathetic towards her sisters
    c. more demanding of Mr. Darcy

Read on:

Pride and Prejudice, written by Jane Austin in 1813, follows the protagonist of the story, Elizabeth Benet, one of the five sisters of an English family of landed gentry as they deal with issues of marriage, morality and misunderstandings.

The human weaknesses of 'pride' and 'prejudice' are what Elizabeth and Darcy, a wealthy, aristocratic land owner, have to overcome in order to come to terms with each other, fall in love and marry. This captivating story is believed by many to be timeless for its numerable characters, relatability and mainly for the skill with which it is told.

The Count of Monte Cristo

Alexandre Dumas

Thus the day passed away. Edmond felt a sort of stupor creeping over him which brought with it a feeling almost of content; the gnawing pain at his stomach had ceased; his thirst had abated; when he closed his eyes he saw myriads of lights dancing before them like the will–o'–the–wisps that play about the marshes. It was the twilight of that mysterious country called Death!

Suddenly, about nine o'clock in the evening, Edmond heard a hollow sound in the wall against which he was lying.

So many loathsome animals inhabited the prison, that their noise did not, in general, awake him; but whether abstinence had quickened his faculties, or whether the noise was really louder than usual, Edmond raised his head and listened. It was a continual scratching, as if made by a huge claw, a powerful tooth, or some iron instrument attacking the stones.

Although weakened, the young man's brain instantly responded to the idea that haunts all prisoners—liberty! It seemed to him that heaven had at length taken pity on him, and had sent this noise to warn him on the very brink of the abyss. Perhaps one of those beloved ones he had so often thought of was thinking of him, and striving to diminish the distance that separated them.

No, no, doubtless he was deceived, and it was but one of those dreams that forerun death!

Edmond still heard the sound. It lasted nearly three hours; he then heard a noise of something falling, and all was silent.

Some hours afterwards it began again, nearer and more distinct. Edmond was intensely interested. Suddenly the jailer entered.

For a week since he had resolved to die, and during the four days that he had been carrying out his purpose, Edmond had not spoken to the attendant, had not answered him when he inquired what was the matter with him, and turned his face to the wall when he looked too curiously at him; but now the jailer might hear the noise and put an end to it, and so destroy a ray of something like hope that soothed his last moments.

Answer the following questions.

1. As the day passed away, Edmond felt a sense of numbness/excitement which gave him almost a sense of restlessness/peace.

2. What made Edmond feel better physically?

3. When Edmond saw the myriads of lights, he thought he was close to _____.

4. Which word tells us Edmond disliked the animals that were found in the prison? Give one example of these "animals".

5. What made Edmond alert enough to raise his head to listen to the noise?

6. What was, according to Edmond, not creating the noise?
   a. a huge claw
   b. a powerful tooth
   c. a minor earthquake
   d. an iron instrument

7. The word "haunts" is used to describe the idea of freedom because
   a. freedom is what prisoners want the most but cannot have
   b. freedom is a ghost

8. The dream of freedom is one that foreruns death because
   a. death is the consequence of failure to escape
   b. nobody has succeeded in escaping from this prison before

9. Edmond heard something falling and then all was silent. What do you think that something was?

10. Which two words show Edmond was keenly fascinated by the noise?

11. How did Edmond behave during the four days he had prepared to die?

12. Do you think Edmond had been a prisoner for a long time? Explain?

Read on:

The Count of Monte Cristo, an adventurous drama set in France, Italy and islands in the Mediterranean Sea between 1815 and 1838, is one of the masterpieces of French author Alexandre Dumas. The story tells of a man who seeks revenge for his unjust imprisonment and his life mission to deal with his internal conflicts of vengeance, justice, identity, redemption, love and God's will.

Daddy-Long-Legs

Jean Webster

The Letters of
Miss Jerusha Abott
To
Mr. Daddy-Long-Legs Smith

215 Fergussen Hall
24th September

Dear Kind-Trustee-Who-Sends-Orphans-to-College,

Here I am! I travelled yesterday for four hours in a train. It's a funny sensation, isn't it? I never rode in one before.

College is the biggest, most bewildering place–I get lost whenever I leave my room. I will write you a description later when I'm feeling less muddled; also I will tell you about my lessons. Classes don't begin until Monday morning, and this is Saturday night. But I wanted to write a letter first just to get acquainted.

It seems queer to be writing letters to somebody you don't know. It seems queer for me to be writing letters at all–I've never written more than three or four in my life, so please overlook it if these are not a model kind.

Before leaving yesterday morning, Mrs. Lippett and I had a very serious talk. She told me how to behave all the rest of my life, and especially how to behave towards the kind gentleman who is doing so much for me. I must take care to be Very Respectful.

But how can one be very respectful to a person who wishes to be called John Smith? Why couldn't you have picked out a name with a little personality? I might as well write letters to Dear Hitching-Post or Dear Clothes-Prop.

I have been thinking about you a great deal this summer; having somebody take an interest in me after all these years makes me feel as though I had found a sort of family. It seems as though I belonged to somebody now, and it's a very comfortable sensation. I must say, however, that when I think about you, my imagination has very little to work upon. There are just three things that I know:

I.   You are tall.
II. You are rich.
III. You hate girls.

I suppose I might call you Dear Mr. Girl-Hater. Only that's rather insulting to me. Or Dear Mr. Rich-Man, but that's insulting to you, as though money were the only important thing about you. Besides, being rich is such a very external quality. Maybe you won't stay rich all your life; lots of very clever men get smashed up in Wall Street. But at least you will stay tall all your life! So I've decided to call you Dear Daddy-Long-Legs. I hope you won't mind. It's just a private pet name we won't tell Mrs. Lippett.

The ten o'clock bell is going to ring in two minutes. Our day is divided into sections by bells. We eat and sleep and study by bells. It's very enlivening; I feel like a fire horse all of the time. There it goes! Lights out. Good night.

Observe with what precision I obey rules–due to my training in the John Grier Home.
Yours most respectfully,
Jerusha Abott
To Mr. Daddy-Long-Legs Smith

Answer the following questions.

1. Why did Jerusha have a funny sensation travelling on a train?

2. Jerusha finds college a most _____ place because she _____ _____ whenever she leaves her room.

3. What is Jerusha's intention writing the letter to Mr. Smith?

4. Is Jerusha comfortable writing to Mr. Daddy-Long-Legs Smith? Give two reasons for that.

5. An antonym for "serious" is
   a. casual
   b. important
   c. urgent

6. Why are the words "Very Respectful" capitalised?

7. What, according to Jerusha, is the short-coming of the name "John Smith"?

8. What are two reasons for Jerusha to feel good to have someone taking an interest in her?

9. Which line tells us the students' daily activities are governed by the ringing of bells?

10. What does Jerusha compare herself to because she feels so energised in the day?

11. Jerusha comments that she obeys rules with precision. It means she obeys rules
    a. dutifully
    b. doubtfully
    c. occasionally

12. Which will surely not be a name for John Smith?
    a. Mr. Girl-Hater
    b. Mr. Rich-Man
    c. Mr. Very Respectful
    d. Daddy-Long-Legs

Read on:

Set in turn-of-the-century New England, the story *Daddy-Long-Legs* was written in 1912 by American writer, Jean Webster. It follows the protagonist, Jerusha (Judy) Abbot, as she leaves the orphanage to be sent to college by a benefactor whom she has never seen in person but only his elongated shadow, for which she dubs 'Daddy-Long-Legs'.

The book is all the letters that Judy, a cheerful and creative person, writes to her mysterious sponsor who becomes her confidant, sharing her joys and sorrows as she matures to adulthood.

<u>Answers</u>

Note to teachers

1. Some of the questions require students to re-examine the text for answers.
2. Some of the questions require students to think to arrive at an answer.
3. Other questions require common sense and some background knowledge. Answers to these questions are often open-ended (answer for these questions are shown as 'multiple answers accepted').

Adventures of Huckleberry Finn

1. sore toe
2. "flying down the street"
3. he began to think of the fun he had planned for the day
4. b. a simile
5. toys, marbles and trash
6. "Nothing less than a great, magnificent inspiration."
7. to make others think it (whitewashing) was an easy job
8. Ben Rogers ; boat ; Big Missouri
9. his heart was light and his anticipation was high
10. b. the water
11. 2 1 4 3
12. Yes—they seem a fun group to be with
    No—they seem to be a nasty bunch
    (multiple answers accepted)

A Princess of Mars

1. a hundred
2. he has never aged
3. a. True
   b. False
4. a. the writer's belief that he will truly die one day
5. an Arizona cave
6. after he has passed over for eternity
7. resurrection → the rising of the dead
   mortality → the state of being subject to death
   phenomenon → remarkable happening
   chronicle → written record of historical events
   commission → a formal document to vest someone with authority
8. b. alliteration
9. science
10. Mars

11. a. he has very little money left
12. a. fiction

The Wind

1. the wind
2. ladies' skirts across the grass
3. "But always you yourself you hid."
   "I could not see yourself at all . . ."
4. c. personification
5. a. False
   b. True
6. beast
7. c. The wind moves across the lake.
8. a child—he asks, "Or just a stronger child than me?"
9. "O wind, a-blowing all day long,
   O wind, that sings so loud a song!"
10. AA BB CC / DD EE CC / FF GG CC
11. Yes—simple / short / good descriptions of the wind
    No—too simple / too short
    (multiple answers accepted)
12. 'My Shadow'
    'From a Railway Carriage'
    'The Moon'
    'The Swing'
    'The Land of Nod'
    (multiple answers accepted)

The Secret Garden

1. looking forward to ; cross ; disappointed
2. a. She would never tell him the news.
   c. She wouldn't mind if Colin died.
3. "It would serve him right!"
4. hyperbole
5. interested ; curious
6. neat packages ; the cover had been removed
7. Mr. Craven had sent it to her and it looked as if it had had picture-books in it
8. the doll
9. books ; games ; a writing-case ; a gold pen ; an inkstand (any four items)
10. everything was so nice ; Mr. Craven remembered her
11. a. grateful
12. 4 2 3 1

The Little Prince

1. six ; magnificent ; primeval
2. a. prehistoric
3. for digestion
4. "pondered deeply"
5. masterpiece"
6. No—they thought it was a hat
7. geography, history, arithmetic and grammar
   these subjects do not need as much creativity as drawing does / these subjects are more "academic" than drawing (multiple answers accepted)
8. b. Children find grown-ups difficult to love.
9. Yes—he chose another profession and learned to pilot airplanes
10. geography ; he could distinguish China from Arizona / if he got lost in the night, such knowledge would be valuable
11. grown-ups' being concerned with matters of consequence
12. the name of the writer - Antoine de Saint-Exupéry - is a French name

Five Children and It

1. business ; Granny ; unwell/sick
2. No—there were bits of paper and string on the floor left over from the packing, and not yet cleared up
3. to have something to do ; to pretend it's seaside ; there are shells there thousands of years old (any two reasons)
4. the gravel-pit and the chalk-quarry
5. a. a simile
6. "the lamb" ; "Baa" was the first thing he ever said
7. No—it seems silly when you read it
   Yes—when you say it, it sounds a little like her name
8. a. was large and wide ; c. had piles of gravel in the sides of the basin
9. there is swishing tide coming in to fill up the moat and wash away the drawbridge and, at the happy last, to wet everybody up to the waist at least
10. to dig out a cave to play smugglers in;
    No—they thought it might bury them alive
11. they would be walking with their heads hanging down into the air
12. d. Children at Play

Bambi's Children

1. a roe deer
2. they felt/said she spoiled her children
3. the crows
4. mother and son (child)
5. she ran faster than he did

6. b. a bad-tempered person
7. opposite / female
8. a shower of dewdrops
9. No—it's a winding path
10. Gurri ; she ; her ; games
11. a. → iii. critically
    b. → ii. gently
    c. → i. disrespectfully
12. b. onomatopoeia

Rebecca of Sunnybrook Farm

1. She's frail, broken and white now.
2. Rebecca's arms
3. c. metonym
4. there's still bitterness in Rebecca
5. "chokingly"
6. She had a quick temper and a sharp tongue.
7. a. True
    b. False
    c. True
8. a. money and means
9. Aunt Miranda had given up her own luxuries and pleasures
10. when Aunt Miranda died ; "willed"
11. a. gratitude
    c. generosity
12. Being Grateful ; The Amazing Rebecca ; Rebecca and Aunt Miranda
    (multiple answers accepted)

Donal That Was Rich and Jack That Was Poor

1. Donal's mother-in-law
2. through the little spy holes
3. a. mothers-in-law
    b. beef
    c. excuses
    d. spy-holes
4. "Jack said he was very welcome to put in ten chests if he liked."
5. No—Jack and his wife first talked over one thing and another
6. a. a full supper
7. Jack said he'd like to know what Donal had in that chest
8. No—he went to a locksmith, got the loan of a whole bundle of keys and tried them all in the chest till he got one that opened it
9. "lost little time"

10. empty bottles, clean-picked bones and the old woman
11. a. suspicion
    b. provision
    c. starvation
    d. deserving
12. for Donal's mother-in-law to pay her way in the next world

Around the World in Eighty Days

1. No—"far from being discouraged"
2. No—"if he had to resort to Macao"
3. a. ignored
4. if his honour was looking for a boat
5. pilot-boat
6. a. voyage
   b. an excursion
7. he could not believe what he heard – going to Yokohama on a pilot-boat
8. a. False
   b. True
   c. False
9. a hundred pounds per day, and an additional reward of two hundred pounds if he reached Yokohama in time
10. to gain a large sum and yet venturing so far
11. a. He did not want to risk his own life.
    b. He did not want to risk the lives of his men.
    c. He did not want to lose his little boat.
    d. They could not reach Yokohama in time.
12. to make the voyage sound a bit shorter / to convince the sailor to take the offer

Chatterer the Red Squirrel Runs for His Life

1. no excitement
2. He danced around, called Bobby names and made fun of him.
3. Coon couldn't catch him if he should try
4. "running for his life"
5. Yes—he knows all about it / he has run for his life often
6. a. Bowser the Hound
   b. Reddy Fox
   d. Old Man Coyote
7. fear and hope
8. fear ; he did not know where to go
9. Shadow was so slim
10. a. repetition
    b. interjection
11. sobbed

12. He regretted that he had not minded his own business and kept his tongue still.
    Yes—his name is Chatterer the Red Squirrel which means he talks a lot

The Phoenix and the Carpet

1. cedar-wood ; eucalyptus oil ; camphor
2. clean tea-cloths
3. "wildly"
4. Robert's tea-cloth caught the golden egg and whisked it off the mantlepiece, and it fell into the fender and rolled under the grate.
5. interjection ; disbelief
6. an egg glowing in a nest of hot ashes
7. a. False
   b. True
8. between the water-butt and the dustbin
9. "and cook refused to lend the kitchen ones (tongs)"
10. four times ; she wanted everyone to see what she saw / she believed something was going to happen
11. "Every mouth was a-gape, every eye a-goggle."
    a flame-coloured bird that was growing bigger and bigger
12. True - the children playing with fire
    Untrue - the bird growing big in no time / the bird can talk

The Old Wife and the Ghost

1. b. a narrative poem
2. No—she lived all alone
3. the full moon
4. b. inversion
5. deaf ; boot ; simile
6. on the larder shelf
7. "But still as a sack the old soul lies"
8. d. pickle
9. mischievous ; he wants to scare the old wife
   angry ; he fails to scare the old wife
   (multiple answers accepted)
10. when the first cock crows / at dawn ; ghosts are believed to be afraid of daylight/light
    (multiple answers accepted)
11. a cat ; to keep the mice away
12. a. entertain

Marcus or, The Boy-Tamer

1. b. much trouble
2. a. True
   b. False
3. fighting with his former teacher
4. fight with
5. a. stopped
6. subdued
7. a townsman of Harrison
8. c. were very strict with him
9. sent him away to school
10. the boy's face and clothes were stained, and the wall, floor and seats were soiled
11. the teacher
12. False ; there was also the cost of the trial

The Story of the Second Old Man, and the Two Black Dogs

1. the writer and the two black dogs
2. to travel in foreign countries for the sake of merchandise
3. No—the brother had to remind him and he had to look closely
4. a beggar
5. 1000 sequins
6. "dissuade" ; No
7. They went to the merchant repeatedly for five years.
8. a. praise ; d. compliment
9. in a corner of his house
10. b. alliteration
11. Yes—they "did a great trade"
12. they are stubborn / they keep asking for money / they are too dependent on others
    (multiple answers accepted)

The Coming of Pollyanna

1. telegram
2. the twenty-fourth of June
3. No—there wasn't a mirror and there were no drapery curtains at the windows or pictures
   on the wall
4. an oven
5. the windows
6. a. False
   b. False
7. No—"The telegram says, 'light hair, red-checked gingham dress and straw hat.' That is all
   I know, but I think it is sufficient for your purpose."
8. four times ; anxious

9. Yes—she sent her flat iron with a vicious dig across the dish-towel as she was ironing
10. one ; "my onliest niece"
11. Yes—it was sometimes said in the town that if Old Tom was Miss Polly's right-hand man, Timothy was her left
12. old days ; a telegram was used to send messages and the open buggy was used for transportation

The Pied Piper of Hamelin

1. "But nothing was done."
2. There were more rats than there was rubbish.
3. They ate anything they could get their teeth on.
4. nervously
5. A large hole would be dug on the outskirts of Hamelin and all the rubbish and rats that could be found and killed would be swept in.
6. c. There was a plague.
7. 4 2 1 3
8. from a hole they hung an effigy that looked remarkably like the Lord Mayor in his black robes and his gold chains
9. b. "No rats or no Mayor!"
10. he was surrounded by his councillors
11. Yes—a magnificent reward
12. d. the silver pipe (found in the 'Read on' section)

Pride and Prejudice

1. air ; exercise
2. she wanted to avoid Mr. Darcy
3. False ; True
4. "with a look of proud calm"
5. Elizabeth → b. was being handed a letter.
   → c. read the letter as requested.
   Mr. Darcy → a. had the letter written in Rosings.
   → d. wrote the letter at eight o'clock in the morning.
7. No—there were two sheets of paper, and they were completely covered in handwriting
8. c. to explain what had transpired between Darcy and Elizabeth
9. a matter of justice
10. Darcy had separated Mr. Bingley from Elizabeth's sister, and Darcy had ruined the hopes of Wickham
11. Darcy had often seen Mr. Bingley in love before
12. Miss Bennet's look and manner were open, cheerful and pleasing as ever, but he saw no sign of strong feeling
13. a. less burdened by unclarified thoughts

The Count of Monte Cristo

1. numbness ; peace
2. the gnawing pain at his stomach had ceased, and his thirst had abated
3. death
4. "loathsome" ; rats / cockroaches / spiders / lizards (multiple answers accepted)
5. abstinence had quickened his faculties ; the noise was really louder than usual
6. c. a minor earthquake
7. a. freedom is what prisoners want the most but cannot have
8. a. death is the consequence of failure to escape
9. a piece of the wall structure / a stone or rock or brick
10. "intensely interested"
11. not speaking to the attendant, not answering the attendant when he enquired what was the matter with him, and turning his face to the wall when the attendant looked too curiously at him
12. Yes—his numbness to life / his wanting to die / his seeing myriads of lights dancing (hallucination)

Daddy-Long-Legs

1. she never rode in one before
2. bewildering ; gets lost
3. to get acquainted with Mr. Daddy-Long-Legs Smith
4. No—she says it feels queer / Mr. Daddy-Long-Legs Smith is someone she doesn't know / she has never written more than three or four letters in her life (any two reasons)
5. c. casual
6. to stress the importance of being very respectful
7. it has little personality
8. as though she had found a sort of family, and as though she belonged to someone now
9. "Our day is divided into sections by bells."
10. fire
11. a. dutifully
12. c. Mr. Very Respectful